Pirates of the Great Lakes

Greg & Nancy Haggart

Lulu Publishing

PIRATES OF THE

GREAT LAKES

Published by Lulu Publishing

Printed in the United States of America

Cover design and layout by Greg Haggart

Editing by Nancy Haggart

First Edition 2008

ISBN 978-1-4357-1949-1

www.piratesofthegreatlakes.com

Acknowledgements

Argh! Greg & Nancy Haggart would like to acknowledge the following scurvy dogs who have walked the plank in our place and have stood by us in all our pillages.

We want to thank our Lord and Savior Jesus Christ for making this possible. All of our friends and family for supporting us, Marland & Linda Haggart, Larry Casner and Darin & Tanya Mogg. The following libraries, societies and archives: The Coleman Area Library in Coleman, Michigan, The Pere Marquette District Library in Clare, Michigan, The Great Lakes Historical Society and The United States National Archives in Washington, D.C.

A special thanks goes out to all the members and pastors of the Well of Worship, Inc. for their prayers and support during the creation and publication of this book.

And thanks be to you the wonderful people of the State of Michigan that we call home!

- Greg & Nancy Haggart

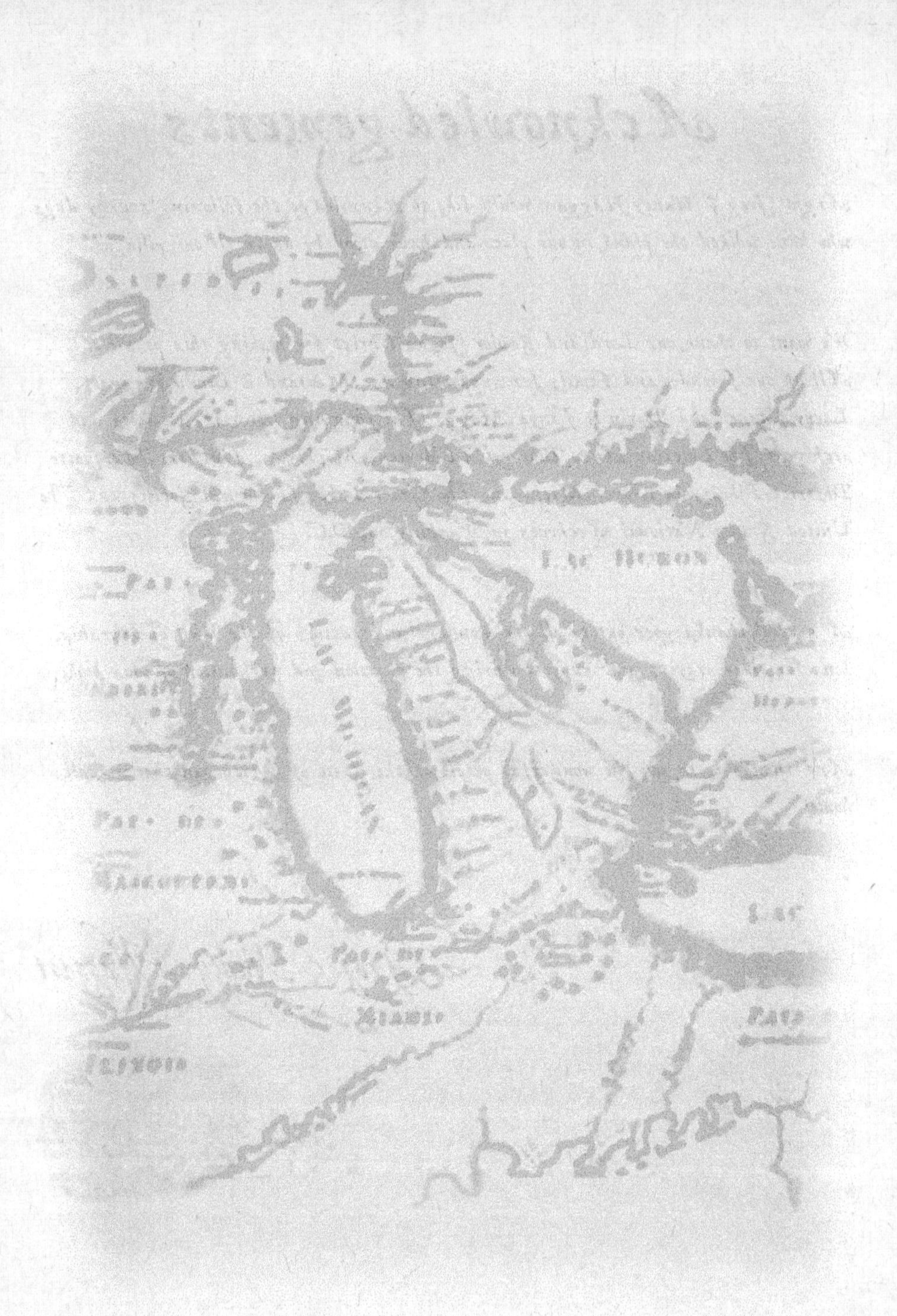

CONTENTS

Vikings set the standard for future pirates by pillaging, exploring and discovering treasure.

INTRODUCTION

Piracy goes back over 3,000 years, rooted from the Middle East regions to Africa and Europe. During those periods the ocean thieves weren't known by the title of Pirate, they were known by another name, Sea Thieves. They were known as outlaws who went outside of civilization's laws of the kingdom, being sea goers enjoying the freedoms of the open sea, alienating themselves from land lovers.

It wasn't until 140 BC that the word peirato was used by the Roman historian Polybius, but it was the Greek historian Plutarch who defined piracy as attacking from the sea by ship. Ancient readers of Homers Iliad and The Odyssey got a taste of what piracy actually was defined as when Homer's characters robbed from sea. However the Norse sailors of the late 8th and 11th century AD were known as Vikings. This term may have come from the Volga River in Russia. The Vikings were traders, warriors and explorers rolled up into one spanning from Russia to Norway, as north as Scotland and Iceland, and are partially credited for discovering North America in the form of Vinland (New Foundland today). Scottish history depicts the Vikings as pillaging coastal towns, robbing farmers and stealing women sailing them off to far regions of the North Sea. Over time piracy grew as exploration picked up. New lands were found along with new riches that fueled the temptation of a life of luxury. However the only way to obtain that dream life was to steal it or ask the sovereign for a quest and take your share of the profit.

As exploration of the Americas began, it was Spain, England and France who had a hand in finding new riches and goods. Exploration became so incredibly tight that rather risk war to take the other side's land and valuables, monarch's commissioned people to do the dirty work for them. These sailors would obtain a letter of marque (a license to pillage) and set on their way, pillaging and taking treasure. These sailors were known as privateers and would sometimes develop their own fleet to assist in major battles against their country's enemy.

As hostilities between Britain, France and Spain came to a close, the Caribbean letters of marque were no longer offered to privateers. No longer needed for military duty, privateers began to lose wealth as peace treaties silenced the seadogs of war. This prompted privateers to put on a new hat and flag and the Golden Age of Piracy began in 1713. Even though the most famous piracy of that age stemmed from the Caribbean, pirates were also sailing the Indian Ocean, Europe and African Coasts.

History seekers and story buffs are often bombarded by pirate lore from the Caribbean. These thieves of the high seas made piracy famous and well known throughout the world. They've excited the imaginations of our children as they run into the backyard with their friends climbing up the side of the hull to stand at the helm of the tree house. Famous stories like Peter Pan and Treasure Island presented a magical depiction and romance to piracy.

This vast area of the Caribbean was easy to get lost in if you didn't know how to sail it, but there was a vast land locked area that is along the American-Canadian border. This area is known as the Great Lakes and is often taken for granted by outsiders who do not understand the region's legends and lore. The lakes are actually inland seas and though they look small on maps, they are very vast and hold colossal mysteries. These inland seas known as Lake Michigan, Lake Superior, Lake Huron, Lake St. Clair, Lake Erie and Lake Ontario don't contain palm trees and glamorous temperatures like the Caribbean Sea, but they do hold true to many legends and adventures in the regions history. Most of the well known ship wrecks these lakes hold stem from the first ship to sail on the lakes known as Le Griffon to the famous ship wreck the Edmund Fitzgerald. For this fact the inland seas of the Great Lakes are much more violent than the oceans. An old Indian legend claims that a person must respect Lake Superior or else she'll take you under. For this reason the autumn months are the most violate times for sailing on the Great Lakes and many sailors from Minnesota to Ontario and also to New York have failed to heed the Indian warnings about the lakes.

But the lakes have held an even darker side throughout the ages that have not only developed into ghost ship stories and ship wreck tails, but talk about explorers, privateers and even pirates. Unknown to many, the Great Lakes was a region that held many pirates from the French and Indian War to the American Civil War and on to the turn of the 20th century. These pirates didn't loot for gold and treasure like most of the Caribbean pirates. Their treasure was timber, women, fish, supplies and whiskey. Seamlessly, these pirates appeared to be immune to the Great Lakes violent nature, being protected by man's carnal nature of riches and women.

Sure the Caribbean was an important region for trade, sugar, tea and other items. In fact much of the American Revolution was fought near the islands in the Caribbean by the British and French. When the British general Cornwall was stationed in Yorktown, Virginia it was a French fleet that was stationed in the Caribbean that forced Cornwall to surrender. This fleet sailed north by way of the Chesapeake Bay ending the war and creating a new nation.

So important were the Great Lakes that Americans, British, Indians and even Confederates fought for control. Read the legend of one Caribbean pirate who saw the advantages of the Great Lakes riches where the other Buccaneers did not!

You've heard about the Caribbean pirates of old, now read about the pirates of the Great Lakes region and there stories of fame and fortune!

Mysterious Travels of the Colby Pirates

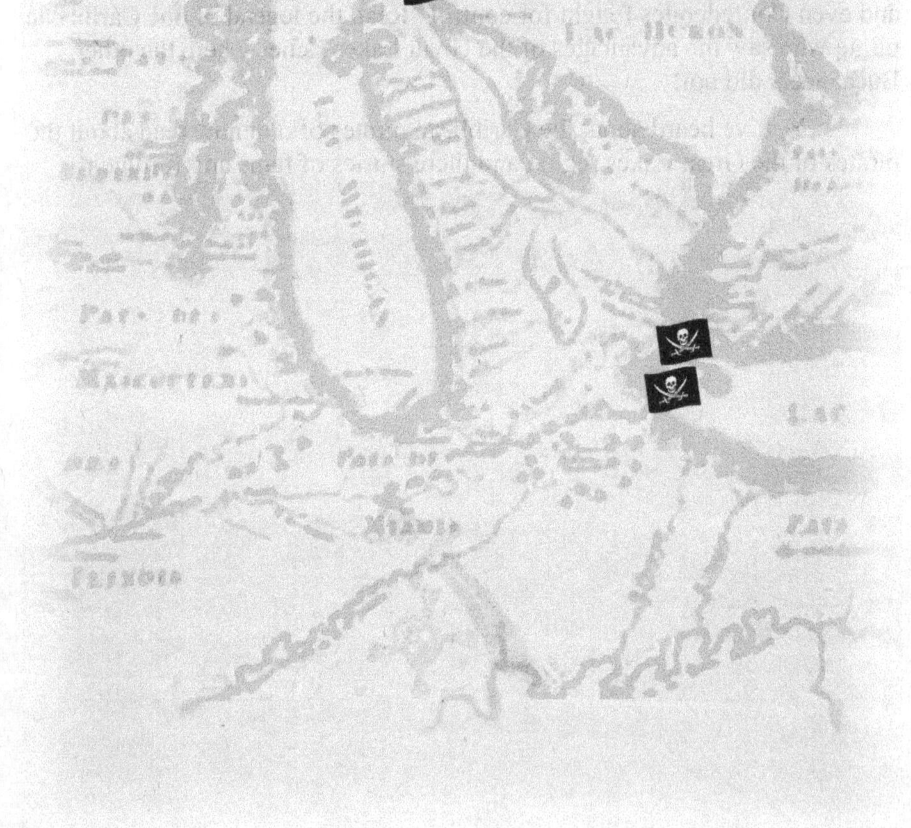

George Colby and the Colby Pirates

On July 24, 1701 a forty-five year old French soldier by the name of Antoine de la Mothe Cadillac founded a piece of land between Lakes St. Clair and Erie. He called this area of land in the French term le détroit (meaning the straits) which is now Detroit, Michigan. Cadillac convinced King Louis XIV's chief minister, Count Pontchartrain to build settlements in the strait region of Detroit. By doing so the French now had a strategic advantage in controlling the upper Great Lakes region, whereby securing their claim on the lakes from the British. The French quickly reinforced Fort Michilimackinac to the north at the Straits of Mackinac to secure their fur-trading empire. Later the French built forts at what is now Niles and Sault Ste. Marie. The French now had complete control over the Great Lakes and shipping routes which lined the pockets of many French merchants.

King George III commissioned George Colby for privatizing on the Great Lakes frontier to disrupt French commerce.

However during the French and Indian War the British and French, along with their Indian allies, fought over control of the Ohio country which spanned the Appalachian Mountains and the Mississippi River. From the Great Lakes to the Gulf of Mexico the two empires met battling it out for control of North America. The regions now known as Michigan and Ontario were under the banner of New France. The British knew that the control of the Great Lakes would be a vital turning point in the war but the French controlled the region with forts lined at every strait. The region of Michigan was a crucial piece of land for the French in order to hold on to control of North America. Michigan to this day still holds many French traditions, such as fudge making, which is still popular near the Straits of Mackinac. There are also many cities in Michigan that have French names such as Au Gres, Mackinac,

Charlevoix and Leelanau.

As hostilities developed into the French and Indian War in North America (1754-1763) King George III came to power and commissioned George Colby as a privateer in the Great Lakes frontier. His duty was to disrupt French shipping and fur-trading along French and British colonies. From New York to the Great Lakes there were over 200 privateers that disrupted French commerce but George Colby is the only known privateer on the Great Lakes to disrupt the trade.

Privatizing in the Great Lakes was much different than Caribbean privatizing and many privateers operated differently than others. Not much is known about George Colby and his band of privateers on the Great Lakes. What is known is that Colby and his men planted false light beacons on the lakes that made French traders run their ships aground. George Colby and his men did not have tall ships like the Caribbean pirates but what they did by tactics they made up for their small size. Colby and his men would wait for the French ships to run aground then they would row up along side of the merchant ships in large boats. The privateers would then board the ship and take what supplies and items they could find to disrupt French shipping on the Great Lakes. The way they handled their privatizing labeled them pirates by the French and earned them the title The Colby Pirates so properly named after their leader George Colby. When the war was over by the signing of the Treaty of Paris, King George III disbanded the Colby Pirates ending piracy on the Great Lakes for a time.

The locations of the Colby Pirate's operations are unknown, but due to colonial expansions of both empires into the Ohio country, it was possible that George Colby and his pirates worked to disrupt shipping of French goods in Lakes Ontario and Erie regions. It is possible since Detroit was such a strategic point during the war that the Colby Pirates pillaged and operated on the shores of the Detroit River. Like many of the pirates of the Caribbean, a fine line was drawn on the Great Lakes between privateers and pirates. George Colby and the Colby Pirates were considered privateers by the British but were pirates to the French for their looting and theft of supplies and goods.

The Legend of Captain Juan Eduardo De Rivera

The Legend of Captain Juan Eduardo De Rivera

Surrounded in legend and lore, there was a buccaneer on the Great Lakes named Captain Juan Eduardo De Rivera. A mythical Caribbean pirate by nature, the Captain operated in the Gulf of Mexico and Florida. He sailed with his ex-captain Jose Gasper (better known as Gasparilla) known for his pillage of Tampa, Florida. De Rivera developed, and later moved, his operations to the Great Lakes, looting small towns and cities in Lake Erie, Lake Huron and Lake Michigan. De Rivera saw an opportunity in the Great Lakes where the other Caribbean buccaneers did not. With the overwhelming movement of pirates disrupting merchant lines in the Gulf of Mexico and the Caribbean, De Rivera moved to the Great Lakes to take advantage of the wealth and riches of the region. In 1793, with his ship (the Diamante Negro) and his crew, he set his sights for the lucrative Great Lakes becoming the only shark in the fresh water seas.

De Rivera is best known for his invasion of the city of Cleveland, Ohio in June of 1799, which became the largest pirate invasion of a city in history. At first, De Rivera had problems convincing his crewmen that a day attack would be a better tactical advantage than what they were use to near Florida. Eventually his crew saw the advantage and agreed to follow the captain's plan. Cleveland posed a challenge for De Rivera, but this peaceful lakeshore city was a pirate's dream come true. Cleveland was at the center of fur trade and was littered with wealthy men who placed their riches in the local banks. If that wasn't enough, the city had the largest lakeshore distillery around. There was more whiskey in Cleveland than in De Rivera's home town of Havana and at the center of it all Cleveland was home to the most beautiful women on all the inland seas of the Great Lakes. Any pirate would not have passed up an opportunity like this.

De Rivera learned that the Cuyahoga River was filled with merchant ships along its riverbanks. Upstream was Fort Scranton which could pose a problem. Not only that but deciding on an escape route would also be an issue. De Rivera cleverly planned an invasion in Cleveland on a Saturday morning. He knew that many of the town's people would be sleeping in, hung-over from a night of whiskey luxury.

With his crew, the plan was set and the pillage began with the Diamante Negro docking at what is now called North Coast Harbor which gave an easier landing point. From there the pirates safely raided the city emptying banks, stealing whisky and defiling women. The raid went so unnoticed to the public that most of the cities wealthy families never even knew that their silver was missing. After the invasion the Diamante Negro set sail for a wilderness hide out on the north shore of Lake Erie.

After the pillage of Cleveland, the crew of the Diamante Negro continued to sail the Great Lakes for several more years staying on the Canadian side to avoid capture. Many rumors developed over the end of De Rivera and his crew. Some say that he went back to Florida and the Gulf to continue pillaging. Others claim the crew of the Diamante Negro lived a life of luxury in New York City. Others lay claim that the crew was captured on the Canadian side of the Detroit River. While De Rivera's crew was arrested for piracy, rather than be hanged, De Rivera tied himself to an anchor and went overboard. The same method was used by his old captain in Tampa to avoid capture by the boarding party of the U.S.S. Enterprise. Jose Gasper latched heavy chains onto his waste and threw himself overboard. As a crewman aboard Gasper's ship this method may have been of practice to the Spanish pirate captains of the last 1700's. This method also complies with the Canadian claim that De Rivera went overboard to avoid capture. However, legend has it that De Rivera untied himself from the anchor and swam ashore.

To this day the people of Cleveland, Ohio celebrate a pirate festival of the pillage of Cleveland in honor of Juan Eduardo De Rivera. Ironically the city of Tampa celebrates Jose Casper in just the same fashion for his pillage of the Florida city. The main question that is on the minds of locals is if Juan and his ship had ever existed. De Rivera is only a legend created by tall tales. There are no sources to support the existence of De Rivera or the pillage of Cleveland. However the legend of Juan Eduardo De Rivera makes for a good sailing tale and a great festival to celebrate the untold memories of the pirates who sailed the Great Lakes.

Pirate Kingdom of James Jesse Strang

Strang was the self proclaimed king of Beaver Island and leader of the Mormon Marauders.

James Jesse Strang, Pirate King of the Mormon Marauders

Historically he is never recognized as a pirate, but much of the actions of James Jesse Strang are reminiscent of piracy. He took over control of a large island on Lake Michigan, was crowned king by his subjects, and ordered all tithes and offerings to be paid to him. After being crowned king of Beaver Island he then claimed the island to be a separate country from the rest of the United States. It was because of James' illegal actions on Lake Michigan that many have claimed it to be piracy. Being isolated for a short time from the mainland of Michigan, James' Mormon marauders would frequently invade isolated coastal settlements and light houses.

After the death of Joseph Smith, Jr. of the Mormon church (The Church of Jesus Christ of Latter Day Saints), Strang claimed to be the successor of the religious sect. Even though having convincing proof that Smith wrote a letter making Strang his successor, (which was later believed to be forged) many of the Mormon congregation followed Brigham Young. Strang was able to convince many of the Mormon's, that did not like Brigham Young's leadership, that he received visions from God. The visions Strang claimed to receive declared that God prepared a place for the Mormons in Wisconsin and that they were going to crown him king.

Since at a young age Strang had admired Napoleon and the English monarchy, he had felt that his destiny was to be a king. Strang got his chance by leading a few Mormon's to Beaver Island where he was finally crowned king over the entire island. At 10:00 A.M. hundreds of Mormon's flocked to the tabernacle and witnessed an aluminum crown being placed on Strang's head by George J. Adams. Strang wore a robe of red flannel, trimmed with white flannel with black specks.

As he held his hand made wooden scepter, Strang told the crowd that he was a Jew and how God had told him in a vision to lead the Israelites. The people gave cheers to their new sovereign and began to live and treat the island as their own country. Eventually more Mormons came to live on the island, ultimately rooting out the previous islanders the Mormons called gentiles. These gentiles hated the Mormons with a passion and did not like the idea of being under the rule of Strang. The government treated Strang's coronation and claiming of Beaver Island as treason and Strangs' popularity grew.

By being crowned king, Strang became the only crowned monarch in American history and began to control shipping routes passing through the waters of the Beaver Islands. Strang's rule over the Beaver Islands and his subjects began to take on a diabolical nature. The leader ordered all tithes to be paid to him and when anyone on the Islands did not pay their tithe he would send men out to their home to retrieve it. Ships passing by the Islands were run aground by fake lighthouses. The Mormon Marauders would climb aboard the ships and murder everyone aboard. The women that were aboard would be spared and taken to live on the islands under Strangs' rule.

As Strang's popularity grew he ran for public office and won. He later ran for re-election and won again. However people living on Beaver Island at the time grew tired of James Jesse Strang and U.S. District Attorney George C. Bates decided to serve an arrest warrant for him on Beaver Island. Bates asked President Filmore for support from the U.S. Navy and was given the Navy's first iron clad twin engine steamer, the USS MICHIGAN. Captain McBlair ordered the MICHIGAN to speed full steam while taking Bates and his U.S. Marshall's to Mackinac Island from Detroit in forty-eight hours. With arrest warrant in hand to have Strang stand before Judge Ross Wilkins in District Court in Detroit, Bates was on his way from Mackinac to end the reign of James Jesse Strang.

The Mormon Marauders had to be stopped. These outlaws were plundering several villages and light houses murdering lighthouse keepers and killing everyone on the ships they boarded. The daughters of ship captains would bare witness to their father's death at the hands of the marauders. At one point Strang had married a young daughter of a captain that died at his marauder's hands.

Strang's downfall as a monarch came to an end when he ordered several decrees and ordered whippings of a few of his subjects that did not comply. These subjects found revenge on June 16, 1856 when two men ambushed Strang, shot him and struck the Mormon leader three times.

The assailants fled to the MICHIGAN where they were cared for by officers. The captain of the MICHIGAN even sent marines to bring their families on board. The MICHIGAN set sail for Mackinac Island where the attackers were greeted with whiskey, cigars and cheers. Later the attackers, Thomas Bedford and Alexander Wentworth, were placed in unlocked cells and went before a justice of the peace where they were then fined $1.25 for court costs. On July 9, 1856, after being taken to safety by his subjects and being evicted from Beaver Island, Strang died from his wounds and is believed to be buried in Voree, Wisconsin.

Even though James Jesse Strang isn't mentioned in history as a pirate, only his actions would seem to present him as one. His legacy may have ignited the idea of a pirate king in many pirate stories, even the Pirates of the Caribbean movies. This is due to the fact that it was Mormon Marauders who pillaged villages and lighthouses and obeyed a king from the inland seas.

Early Voyages of Bully Hayes

Bully Hayes, Pirate of the South Seas.

Captain Bully Hayes

Bully Hayes was initially regarded as the last of the Buccaneers and is well known for being a pirate on the South Pacific seas. Born in either 1827 or 1829 in Cleveland, Ohio, William Henry Hayes was the son of Henry Hayes, who was an innkeeper or most likely ran a saloon on the banks of the Cuyahoga River. Hayes was inspired at a young age when fur traders, lake captains, lumberjacks and Indians came into the saloon. These rugged types would settle scores with not only fists but guns and knives. The young Hayes would over hear stories told by the lake captains. Tales of freedom on the open inland seas, adventure, women, murder and theft. Just as any child would become inspired by the story of Treasure Island, so had Hayes been when he heard the stories of the captains.

When Hayes reached the age of 20, he took it upon himself to sail the Great Lakes becoming the captain of his own vessel. Over time he began to have a reputation for being a handsome young man. His rippling muscles and dashing good looks earned him a girl in every port. He wasn't without his critics though and was recognized as a womanizer for using his charm to his sexual advantage. He was also a gambler and got into fights nearly everywhere he went. Returning to his home port of Cleveland he helped to establish the city as a hell-raising port.

Over time, while sailing the Great Lakes, Hayes got married but that didn't slow him down from his brutish life style as a sailing captain. Accusations of piracy began to emerge and later he was accused of being involved in a horse stealing scheme that drew the authorities. Hayes left Cleveland for New York where he learned how to sail the open ocean, eventually voyaging around Cape Horn then back north to the western United States anchoring in San Francisco. It was there that Hayes fell in love again and married a second time. Hayes grew attached to the life of San Francisco with its gold miners, cowboys and sailors all living a free and wild life. Law and order wasn't like it was in the east where he grew up. The authorities at a small number compared to the mass population, and many of them were corrupt themselves. Many of the pirates and gamblers took this to their advantage by robbing and cheating the miners out of their gold.

The open seas of the Great Lakes became known as the training grounds for Hayes' Pacific career as a pirate. His so called training was put into motion during a poker game when he was caught using marked cards. One man pulled a knife and stabbed Hayes' hand, pinning it to the table but Hayes' Lake port training instincts allowed him to pull the knife from his hand in record time. After an intense scuffle and a gun being drawn to calm Hayes down, the gamblers tied his hands and cut off his right ear. Hayes roused in rage breaking the rope and with rock hard fists knocked the man out cold. After witnessing Hayes' strength and brut force the other attackers fled in terror.

Hayes took for the adventurous canvas of the Pacific and painted his own adventure like the sea captains back home in Cleveland. His voyages took him to several areas of the Pacific including the Hawaiian Islands where he counterfeited postage stamps. He was reported to have been shipped wrecked near a pacific island where he was nursed back to health by the natives. After recovering, he kidnapped the natives and sold them into slavery. Hayes' black birding of South Sea islanders brought them to work in mines, farms and other hard labor areas of Australia and New Zealand. One source says that he once cleared out a whole island of natives.
He earned the nickname "Bully" for being rude to his crew and to those who were land lovers. However people who were close to Hayes said that one moment he was a saint and the other a demon. Some believed that Hayes was the reincarnation of a true buccaneer, while others claimed that he was an honest man who was the product of circumstance. However history has labeled Hayes as a pirate with stories that describe him as no less than a preacher of the gospel.

Hayes started off being commissioned by several vessel owners in San Francisco to sail their ships across the Pacific to pick up cargo and supplies. Hayes' agenda was very different than what the private ship owners intended. Once in port at his final destination, Hayes would sell the ship and everything on board making a hefty profit. He did this 15 times over the years until finally Hayes got into black birding. Hayes was an excellent navigator and ship captain in the deep ocean of the Pacific, being able to direct his ships through the sharp reefs.

This cover design reveals Hayes' brut force as a pirate.

The first recorded arrival of Hayes in Australia was at Fremantle in January 1857. By this time he was the master of the C.W. BRADLEY, which he obtained by Singapore in the same manner he had intended to cheat the owner by selling the ship and its goods in Australia. On August 25, 1857 at Penwortham, South Australia he married Amelia Littleton. He was later charged with indecent assault of a young girl (charges were later dismissed) on January 1860 in Sydney after he had stolen the ELLENTIA. Hayes was later imprisoned for debt in Darlinghurst but later declared insolvent and was released. He sailed to Hunter Valley and after spending much time there he sailed to New Zealand on the CINCINNATI with his companions. It was there that he met and married Rosa Buckingham. Later in August of 1864, near Nelson, Hayes escaped drowning while Rosa along with her child and brother did not survive.

Finally Hayes bought the RONA in which he became a trader and black birder. One source from an Australian dictionary of biography states that Hayes was married to a new bride at this point, but her name isn't known. Many historians believe that Hayes could have possibly been a Mormon due to his multiple marriages; however no sources are able to back this claim. In these marriages it is believed that Hayes never asked for a divorce, nor traveled back to see his many wives.

While making a trip near Manihiki, Cook Islands, the RONA was lost. Later he joined an American black birder named Ben Pease and sailed with him in the PIONEER. The PIONEER would return to Samoa renamed as the LEONORA and Ben Pease mysteriously gone. Hayes would pick the most beautiful island girls and display them on board in lagoons for men to see. He worked closely with the Chinese pirates and as men came aboard to have some fun with the girls, Hayes would kidnap them and sell them off to the Chinese.

On March 15, 1874 Hayes' adventures on the LEONORA came to an end at Kusaie in the Caroline Islands. The LEONORA struck a reef and was a total lose but her company escaped. There are two different stories on how Hayes got off the islands. One suggests that Hayes set up a trading post and terrorized the natives. When the H.M.S. ROSARIO showed up, many of the natives began complaining to the missionaries about Hayes' violent nature. To avoid capture he took a small boat and went to sea where the American whaler ARCTIC picked him up and sailed to Guam in February of 1875. After being in the Philippines for a time he appeared in San Francisco where he began his last adventure on the ship LOTUS.

Bully Hayes' ship, the Leonora, used to be called the Pioneer and was owned by American black birder Ben Pease.

Another source suggests that while on the Caroline Islands Hayes met with missionaries from the H.M.S. ROSARIO. Hayes subsequently faked accepting Christ as his savior and left with the missionaries to spread the word of God where he finally appeared in San Francisco.

In October of 1876 Captain Bully Hayes sailed his last adventure on the yacht LOTUS where he was seen with another woman which was believed to be the owner's wife. With a crew of two, Hayes sailed for the Marshall Islands where he had several quarrels with a sailor. Sources differ on Hayes death. One source claims that the murderer was a sailor while another suggests it was a cook. However the many versions of his death all agree that Hayes was killed by a blow to the head or a gun shot. Most sources agree that Hayes' body was pushed overboard where it was left to float in the ocean in a watery grave. His murder was reported when the yacht reached Jaluit, Marshall Islands but his murderer has never come to justice.

Raids of Jacob Thompson

Jacob Thompson as U.S. Secretary of the Interior.

Jacob Thompson Confederate Pirate of the Great Lakes

As the American Civil War began, secret operations took place by the Confederate States on the Great Lakes. If they were successful with their operations much, like the war of 1812, the outcome would have resulted in a war between the United States and Canada. It is unknown just how many Confederate pirates were working in secret on the Great Lakes. We do know that they were lead by Jacob Thompson, one of the influential figures of the Civil War.

Jacob Thompson was born on the 15th of May, 1810 in Leasburg, Caswell County in North Carolina. Jacob was a very bright young man and prepared for college at the Hawfield School in Orange County, graduating valedictorian in his class at the University of North Carolina in 1831. He began to study law and performed much of his duties in the courts of North Carolina. Thompson was actively in the affairs of the Native Americans in the U.S. Land Office and the Indian Agency after accepting an invitation from his brother, Dr. James Thompson, to move to the state of Mississippi. He was then elected to the state legislature and later to the U.S. House of Representatives, being reelected to Congress through 1851.

When James Buchanan took office as the President of the United States, Thompson was appointed as the Secretary of the Interior in March 1857. It was during his work as the Secretary of the Interior when he had found out that much of the south was considering secession from the union. As a Mississippian he was alienated from secret military conferences on the pending southern secession. On January 8, 1861 Thompson resigned his position as Secretary of the Interior, and Mississippi withdrew from the union the following day.

When the American Civil War began, Thompson volunteered his services to the newly formed confederacy supplying his personal funds to help equip the Confederate troops. While assisting the training of the new troops he became an aide to General Beauregard at Shiloh and obtained the rank of Lt. Colonel. This active role allowed him to see the battles of Vicksburg, Corinth, Tupelo, Grenada and the Tallahatchie River.

After military operations Jacob returned home to Oxford in late 1863 where he was elected again to the state legislature. In March of 1864 Confederate President Jefferson Davis asked Thompson to lead a delegation to Canada which he accepted; arriving in Canada in May of 1864.

Jacob's mission was to be a peaceful diplomat with Canadian political officials, but if he was unsuccessful he was to try and alter the course of the war. One part of that mission would be to arrange an escape of Confederate POW's on Johnson's Island. Johnson's Island is off the coast of Ohio in Sandusky Bay on Lake Erie. This Union prison was housed by roughly 3,000 Confederate prisoners of war but had the ability to hold 5,000.

A Confederate headquarters was set up in The Queen's Hotel on Toronto Bay. The leading Canadian newspapers published favorable articles on the southern operations of the American Civil War, which boosted the morale of Thompson's men. However Confederate operations that took place outside of the borders of the Confederacy weren't very favorable to the Northern States at the time. There have been stories of cavalry raids, and privateers on the high seas that the Northern States saw as raiders, marauders, looters and even pirates. There were even reports that described Confederates capturing and burning two small steamers on Lake Erie, but these reports cannot be confirmed. Rumors spread throughout many of the lake states that Confederates were operating in the Great Lakes.

Confederate Captain John Yates Beall wrote:

"Immediately on my arrival in Canada I went to Colonel Thompson at Toronto...He informed me of a plan to take the Michigan (14 guns) and

release the Confederate officers confined at Johnson's Island...We arranged our plans...I came to Windsor to collect men...On Monday morning we started..."

The U.S.S. Michigan in later years.

The plot to rescue the Confederate POW's on Johnson's Island was to play out on September 19, 1864, in Malden, Ontario. Beall's mission by order of Thompson was to take the U.S.S. MICHIGAN, that was guarding the prisoners at Johnson's Island, and rescue the Confederates off the Island. Posing as passengers, Captain Beall and his men had taken a steamer at Kelley's Island called the PHILO PARSONS. In the meantime Jacob instructed Captain Charles H. Cole, another Confederate captain, to create a distraction then signal Captain Beall to come in for the attack on the MICHIGAN.

After the PHILO PARSONS had stolen timber off Middle Bass Island and sent it's small steamer, the ISLAND QUEEN, to the bottom of Lake Erie (with her crew stranded on the island) Beall and his crew were full steam ahead for Johnson's Island. When Cole and his men arrived at Johnson's Island to create a distraction he was arrested and Beall never received a signal to attack. Upon arriving at Sandusky Beall's men mutinied when they started to attack the MICHIGAN. The PHILO PARSONS was forced to turn around and head for Sandwich, Ontario. On September 20th, Beall abandoned ship and sank the PHILO PARSONS, possibly due to the MICHIGAN traveling close behind (under the command of Commander John C. Carter).

Commander Carter of the U.S.S. MICHIGAN later reported thinking that Cole was the master mind behind the plot:

"I have got the principal agent prisoner on board and many accomplices."

After the PHILO PARSONS disaster all hopes to sway the Northwestern States of Ohio, Indiana and Illinois were ruined. The jig was up after the attempt on Johnson's Island. Regardless of the attention the

PHILO PARSONS caused, Jacob Thompson and Dr. John Bates (an old Mississippi River pilot from Louisville, Kentucky) purchased a new boat called the GEORGIAN for $17,000. The vessel drew much attention as it arrived at Buffalo, New York. The public learned that the Confederates intended to arm her and strengthen her bow making her ready for ramming.

Though the GEORGIAN never carried any supplies or armaments it was subject to many boardings by customs officials. The mayor of Buffalo reported the arrival to the U.S. Navy. Two tugboats were commandeered and fitted with cannons and soldiers in case the GEORGIAN were to attack a target. As the GEORGIAN made its way from Lake Erie to Lake Huron it became impossible for the Confederates to perform any kind of military action.

On December 3rd, Jacob wrote to Confederate Secretary of War Benjamin Judah:

"The bane and curse of carrying out anything in this country is the surveillance under which we act. Detectives or those ready to give information stand at every street corner. Two or three can not interchange ideas without a reporter."

On April 6, 1865 Canadian authorities seized the GEORGIAN in the Georgian Bay. After a thorough search of the vessel, Canadian's found documents revealing intent to use Greek Fire and Confederate Marines to attack and gain control of Union fishing vessels. This would produce a small assembly of a fully operational Confederate navy on the Great Lakes.

After two refits by its new owners in 1874 and 1882 the GEORGIAN went on for 20 additional years sailing the Great Lakes as a freighter. It wasn't until May 9, 1888 while towing the schooner GOLD HUNTER, that the GEORGIAN was damaged by an ice flow. The GEORGIAN is believed to be the only pirate ship lying at the bottom of the Great Lakes.

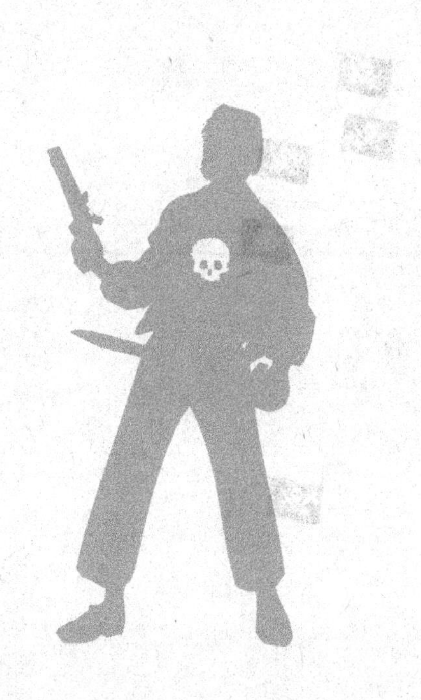

Legendry Voyages of Roaring Dan Seavey

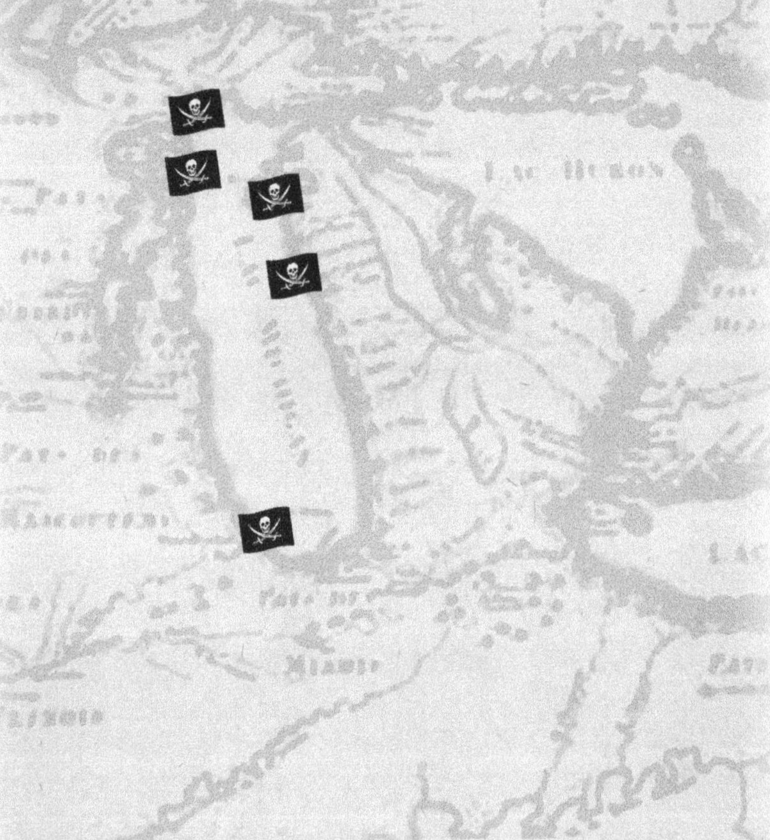

Roaring Dan Seavey was the toughest pirate to sail Lake Michigan.

"Roaring" Dan Seavey

The most well known pirate of Lake Michigan, "Roaring" Dan Seavey earned his nickname Roaring Dan for being a scrapper. Believed to be the only person charged on Lake Michigan with piracy; his antics were legendry. He was tall and stocky and famous for his commerce of illegal liquor, tainted women and fighting style. There are actually more stories told about his legendry theft of the NELLIE JOHNSON than any other story of his life. There was much more to Roaring Dan's career as a pirate than meets the eye.

Dan Seavey was born on March 23, 1865 in Portland, Maine. His youth was filled with a love for the open sea and later ran away to be one with it. When he became old enough he joined the U.S. Navy and gained the experience needed for his unexpected career. He discovered that he would rather give orders than receive them and when his time in the Navy was over he left for the regions of Wisconsin and later Minnesota. While in Wisconsin he worked for a time for the Bureau of Indian Affairs. However one source claims that Seavey lived in Milwaukee for a time starting his own fishing business. One thing that is known about Dan Seavey is that he got married and the couple had a child together. The name of his wife is unknown.

Dan Seavey was someone who was seeking adventure when his buddy Captain Frederick Pabst (who was Milwaukee's brewing master and known for his famous beer by his name) invited him to come to Alaska. By 1898 people from all over the nation were heading up to Alaska for the gold rush. Pabst and Seavey were on a gold mining expedition in the north trying to hit it big. Seavey loved the adventure and could not resist leaving his wife and child for a chance at mining gold. It was probably along the Yukon and Alaska border, that Seavey saw it with his bare eyes, small towns in the style of the old west with saloons, prostitutes and fights. Historically the rush was chaotic as thieves stole thousands of nuggets from the gold miners as they came into town. The artic north became a haven for the darkest of criminals. Seavey and Pabst learned rather quickly the importance of brawling to protect their investments. After Pabst and Seavey's time in the gold rush, Seavey settled near Escanaba, Michigan flat broke and a changed man. He began working for the loggers, miners and iron workers. The iron money the company put out to pay their workers probably didn't appeal to him since it looked like play money. Like in the navy, Seavey didn't take to kindly to taking orders from authority, so he decided to put his sailing knowledge to work and became his own boss. He gathered what income he had and bought a schooner called the WANDERER. He hired a crew and opened a freighting business, but that was never his true intentions. Seavey became a hard man after Alaska and probably saw the other side of mankind and didn't like it. No one is sure what caused a change in Seavey. Something may have happened to him in Alaska that made him want to get back at the world. The freighting business he started was actually a cover for his true intensions. Seavey and his crew of the WANDERER began pillaging port towns at night. They would enter a port without their running lights on and took whatever they wanted. Lumbering was huge so they would even take timber on board. If there were any unattended boats in the ports they would take those also. Pretty much what ever they could get their hands on and what they could sell in Chicago. Seavey even stole animals, from oxen to deer, and sold them on the black market in the windy city. At one point the mob that he sold venison to decided to obtain venison from Summer Island, cutting out the middle man. Seavey wasn't about to have some wise guys entering in on his turf. Chicago was their territory, but Lake Michigan was Seavey's and he liked it that way. If the mob wanted anything from Lake Michigan they had to go through Seavey to get it. He and the crew of the WANDERER cut the hoodlums off half way up Lake Michigan, but the WANDERER withdrew from the fight due to the mobs numbers. The WANDERER later returned equipped with a cannon mounted on the ship. Seavey fired hitting the mob scum sending their ship to the bottom of the lake. The WANDERER never bothered to pick up survivors.

Seavey not only used the WANDERER for smuggling but to sail prostitutes around the lakeshores of the great lakes. Seavey's best profit came when he took advantage of the lumber jacks. The WANDERER would set sail for the nearest lumber camp and invited loggers on board. While the lumber jacks were having their play of the women, Seavey would order the WANDERER to set sail, while the lumber jacks were still on board. When the loggers came out of the cabin from a moment of lust they would find that the ship was out in the middle of Lake Michigan. Seavey and his crew would rob the loggers and throw them over board. Dead men can't tell any tails and unfortunately Seavey and his men got away with it.

Seavey loved to fight and would test anyone who claimed to be the toughest man around. He would invite them to brawl, but he had two conditions during the scrap; no guns and no knives. Sometimes Seavey would resort to biting during a fight to gain some advantage. At one time in a bar in Manistee, Seavey fought a lumberjack that claimed he could beat anyone there. Seavey accepted the challenge and both of them ordered everyone out of the bar. By the time the police arrived they discovered the interior of the bar completely destroyed.

Roaring Dan Seavey was the best scrapper on the lake until one day in Escanaba he entered a bar and discovered a tiny man looking for him. Seavey presented himself and the two began fighting. Seavey's face began to look like ground chuck, and after a few shots of whisky the two went at it again. Seavey found out later his crew hired a professional fighter from Chicago to cut him down to size. When the fight was over, Seavey shouted the famous phrase at the fighter.

"Come back tomorrow, you tubercular brat, and I'll give you another lickin'."

Seavey is definitely a man of legend. There are mixed stories about his activities and the dilema is discerning truth from fiction.

Seavey is best known for his theft of the NELLIE JOHNSON, however there are two stories that surround the legendry endeavor.

The date was June 11, 1908, Seavey and his crew of the WANDERER had arrived in Grand Haven, Michigan. Seavey saw his prize, the schooner NELLIE JOHNSON, with its crew off the ship and drinking in a bar. Seavey entered the bar and drank the crew under the table, and left the bar still sober and boarded the NELLIE JOHNSON only to discover the captain still aboard. Seavey over came the captain and chained him up. Rumor has it in this version of the story that the captain was his old friend Frederick Pabst, but this wasn't true. The legend tells that Seavey sailed the schooner out on Lake Michigan where he dumped his old friend, then sailed off to Chicago where he sold the boat and all its materials and supplies.

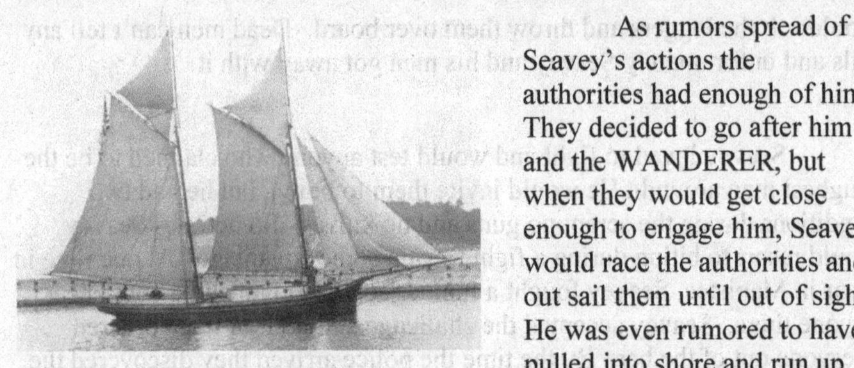

The Nellie Johnson made the run between Beaver Island and the mainland.

As rumors spread of Seavey's actions the authorities had enough of him. They decided to go after him and the WANDERER, but when they would get close enough to engage him, Seavey would race the authorities and out sail them until out of sight. He was even rumored to have pulled into shore and run up the country side, out running the authorities, then got back on the lake and sailed away. They just could not capture the pirate, so the authorities devised a plan to put him in irons. One of the officers went undercover as a yacht owner, and asked Seavey to captain his yacht to Mackinac Island, which Seavey gladly accepted. However, as the yacht began to sail the lake, the revenue cutter TUSCARORA was waiting. Seavey spotted the revenue cutter and at nightfall a race began. Sighting the port of Frankfort he began to sail for it, he strategically placed a beacon forcing the TUSCARORA to run aground. Not willing to lose this race the crew of the TUSCARORA fired a warning shot across the bow of the yacht and Seavey surrendered to the authorities to wait trial in Chicago. Seavey was later released because there was no sign of the NELLIE JOHNSON'S captain. Seavey claimed in court that the captain of the NELLIE JOHNSON gave him the boat to pay off a debt he owed to him. Of course that side of the story is the legend.

However, historically that isn't how the story went. This was a tail that was told by sailors on the lake. Much like telling it through the grape vine, Seavey's legend became twisted and fell into lore. The actual captain of the NELLIE JOHNSON was R.J. McCormick who had actually informed the authorities that it was Seavey who stole his ship. The truth is Seavey actually could not sell the NELLIE JOHNSON to anyone in Chicago.

According to the Chicago Daily Tribune, June 30, 1908, Seavey and two of his men boarded the NELLIE JOHNSON and sailed out to sea to try and sell her for the green stuff. McCormick squealed and informed the authorities that his ship was stolen by Seavey. After failing to sell the NELLIE JOHNSON and its cargo, Seavey sailed back to his home in Frankfort, Michigan where he moored her in a river. The authorities caught wind of this and sent Captain Preston H. Ueberroth to apprehend Seavey.

Ueberroth took the steam ship TUSCARORA up the lake to Seavey's place in Frankfort, however by morning Seavey had set sail on the lake in the WANDERER. Seavey spotted the TUSCARORA, caught some wind in his sail and the race was on; steam vs sail. In the end Seavey was captured and taken to Chicago to await trial. Many sources believe that Seavey was brought up on charges of piracy and became the only person "charged" with piracy on the Great Lakes. Unfortunately those stories are just part of the ever growing legend of "Roaring" Dan Seavey. He was never charged with piracy. When the trial of the theft of the NELLIE JOHNSON was over, Seavey was brought up on charges of stealing a ship. However, with a good attorney Seavey got off and the case was dismissed.

In 1918 Seavey lost the WANDERER which was destroyed by fire, but he replaced her with a 45-foot motor launch (which came in handy during the prohibition period.) Rather than attempt to capture Seavey again and risk the loss of life, the authorities made Seavey an honorary U.S. Marshall. Seavey took it to heart for a little while, by hauling in some of the worst smugglers on the Great Lakes dead or alive. The crime rate was actually down on the lakes because of Seavey, but like all good things there had to be an end. Seavey took off the badge and began making more money by smuggling than by enforcing the law.

When Seavey was in his elderly years children began to touch his heart. He would allow children on board his ship wherever he came to port, telling stories and legends of his adventures on the lakes. He considered all the children who boarded his ships to be his crewmen. Over his life as a pirate on Lake Michigan, the criminal life allowed him to obtain millions of dollars. However he gave much of his wealth away to the poor and charities for children. By his act of kindness and repentance he became a modern day Robin Hood. In 1949 at the age of 84 in a nursing home in Prestigo, Wisconsin, Seavey died. His life as a pirate was well forgotten in history, but his legend will live on as the longest living pirate in history.

The River Pirates of Two Rivers

The Fox Gang

During the lumbering age, there was a group of river pirates dubbed the Fox Gang. This twelve man gang operated in the settlement of Two Rivers, Wisconsin; which is located on the west shore of Lake Michigan. At the time Two Rivers was a lumbering town. Along their coast was an assortment of white pine, hemlock, oak, maple, beech and birch. These trees were used for making shingles or stave which were very valuable in the market due to their perfection with straight grain and no knots or blemishes.

The Fox Gang ran their dirty operation on the water. They would canoe down the river in search of pines fit for shingles and staves. Piling the bolts on the shore, they awaited the return of the crew. The bolts were then brought down to the men who made the shingles and staves. They were even known to pick up a bolt here and there that already had another brand on it. All it took was a cut of the brand and no one could tell the difference. If someone complained, the boys would just work him over and maybe throw him in the river. With their pockets full and feeling especially rowdy, the Fox Gang would come into the small town and terrorize the locals. The western cowboys were teddy bears compared to these river pirates.

Finally, in 1849, the townspeople had had enough and elected a man named McCullum as their constable. They were confident that he could either make the gang cool off or leave. In all, the townspeople hoped that McCullum would bring Fox and his gang before the justice of the peace (Justice Peterson) to await a hearing.

One day the gang traveled near a little brewery owned by Edward Muellar. One of the gang members spotted a flag pole out front of the brewery and bet Fox that he couldn't shimmy up the pole and grab the flag. The flag pole was placed there by the late Richard Muellar when he was just a boy at the age of ten, but that didn't matter to Fox as he took the bet and started up the pole. Fox didn't get even ten feet up the pole before it broke sending him into a puddle of mud. The whole gang created such an up roar that a flock of geese started in giving a shout. Fox quickly grabbed a club and began beating the geese to death. When Edward Muellar (the brewer) arrived he witnessed Fox killing off his prized geese and asked Fox what was the matter. Fox replied that the dead geese had laughed at him for falling in the puddle. Edward Muellar thought Fox had gone mad and ran to the defense of his geese. Fox struck Muellar knocking him out cold. The gang quickly ran for it and dispersed in several directions. When Muellar woke, he went before Justice Peterson and described to him what had happened. Peterson quickly sent out a warrant for the arrest of Fox, and Constable McCullom rounded up a posse and begun the search for the river pirate.

At around nine o'clock at night, Constable McCullom found Fox held up in one of the shanties in which shingles were made. Fox was in a drunken daze. McCullom shook his shoulder and told him he was under arrest and to come quickly. Fox rose as if to come without complaint but then suddenly shoved a knife toward McCullom. The constable was expecting such an attack and swung to the side, but not before securing a dangerous wound. Fox ran out the door but was greeted by one of the posse. A larger than life German by the name of Linstedt, who told him to drop the knife or he would kill him. Seeing his confronter's seriousness, Fox dropped the weapon and was escorted to Justice Peterson right away. While on trial, in a small shanty nearby, Fox had a quiet and submissive demeanor. Consequently, he had a request to go to a privy not far way. The request was granted but only with a guard. It was an intensely a dark night and Fox was able to slip away from the guard and was never seen again. Most of his gang soon disappeared also.

Shivering Timber Pirates

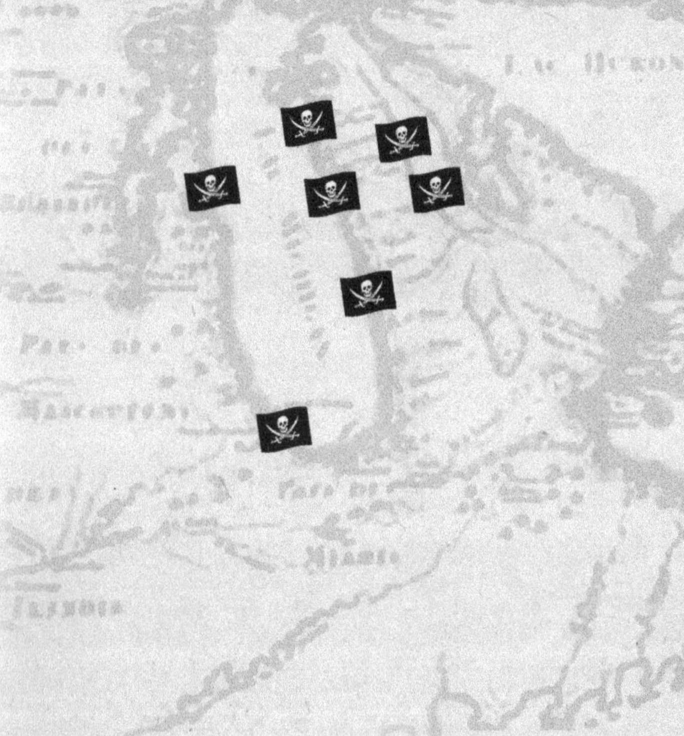

Timber Pirates

When the French and Indian War came to a close, much of the land that was once New France came into the possession of the British Empire. These forests ranging from the Ohio Valley to what is now Wisconsin and Michigan were important to much of the British ship building industry. What was more important were the tall trees that could be used to replace the broken masts during sea battles. The French used the forests of the Ohio Valley and the Great Lakes to make trading posts and forts, while the British and later Americans used the lumber for merchant and war ships. It is believed that the massive naval power that the British had constructed was credited to the vast forests of North America.

During the period of British control of North America, the monarchy would send personnel out in the forests of the colonies, and mark important trees with the king's seal. It was important at the time to find good tall trees for masts and strong timber to build ships. By having a vast amount of timber the British could produce ship after ship to build and maintain the empire. People who cut the king's trees down would be put on trial. When the American Revolution came to a close the new government of the United States claimed all property that belonged to the king of England. However the forests were very large taking up miles of land. By the 1800's, to protect much of the forest area and keep it under government control, Congress passed laws only allowing the lumber companies to take forty acres at a time. The lumber barons began to get smart and allowed their men to take what was dubbed Round 40's, by cutting down a 40 acre area then continue cutting around the 40. By doing this they were breaking the law and taking what wasn't theirs. The government finally stepped in by sending timber agents, but the regions were too large for the small group of men to patrol and enforce the law. The agents asked for assistance from the USS MICHIGAN to stop the lumber ships and assist in serving warrants. Most lumber barons began ordering their men to keep cutting while the agents instructed them not to. As the illegal timber was moved onto timber ships the crews themselves became outlaws; sailing with illegal cargo. The USS MICHIGAN was successful in stopping most of the shipping but many got away. With the vast forests in Wisconsin and Michigan it became a lost cause for the timber agents. Many times the agents had trouble even trying to find the locations of the lumberjacks due to the vast forests.

Lumberjacks from Clare, Michigan.

The times were hard during the big lumber age, so much so that Clare County, Michigan had the highest causality rate for lumberjacks. The county's seat of the City of Harrison became known as the brawling capital for lumberjacks. Most of the men would visit the region to find a fight in order to test their manhood.

Lumber companies often stole lumber from other companies. Some lumber companies would send their lumberjacks to move in on another companies and steal all their newly cut timber. Some would even block whole rivers off from the other lumber companies taking their lumber in the process. One such event happened in Muskegon, Michigan. Legendry "Silver Jack" Driscose (who was a grizzly bear size of a man but was a teddy bear to those who knew him) was asked to walk over to the other company and lick their best man settling the dispute. Silver Jack beat the sap out of the lumber king's best man. Silver Jack always picked the men up after a fight, and took them over his shoulder and hauled them off to the bar. There they would have a few drinks to cut the pain.

Silver Jack was never considered to be a timber pirate like many of the shivering timber bandits, but he was the perfect example of a true lumber jack and how things were back in those days.

When the lumbering age died out so to did timber piracy. Small towns and farm fields replaced nature's skyscrapers, and the rails that once supported the lumber companies turned a bright eye on society. As more cities and fields replaced forests, the rail companies began offering more transportation opportunities for American citizens. With the growth of commerce and the rails across the Great Lakes regions, the inland seas began to see more recreation and new endeavors for pirates.

Sea Theives

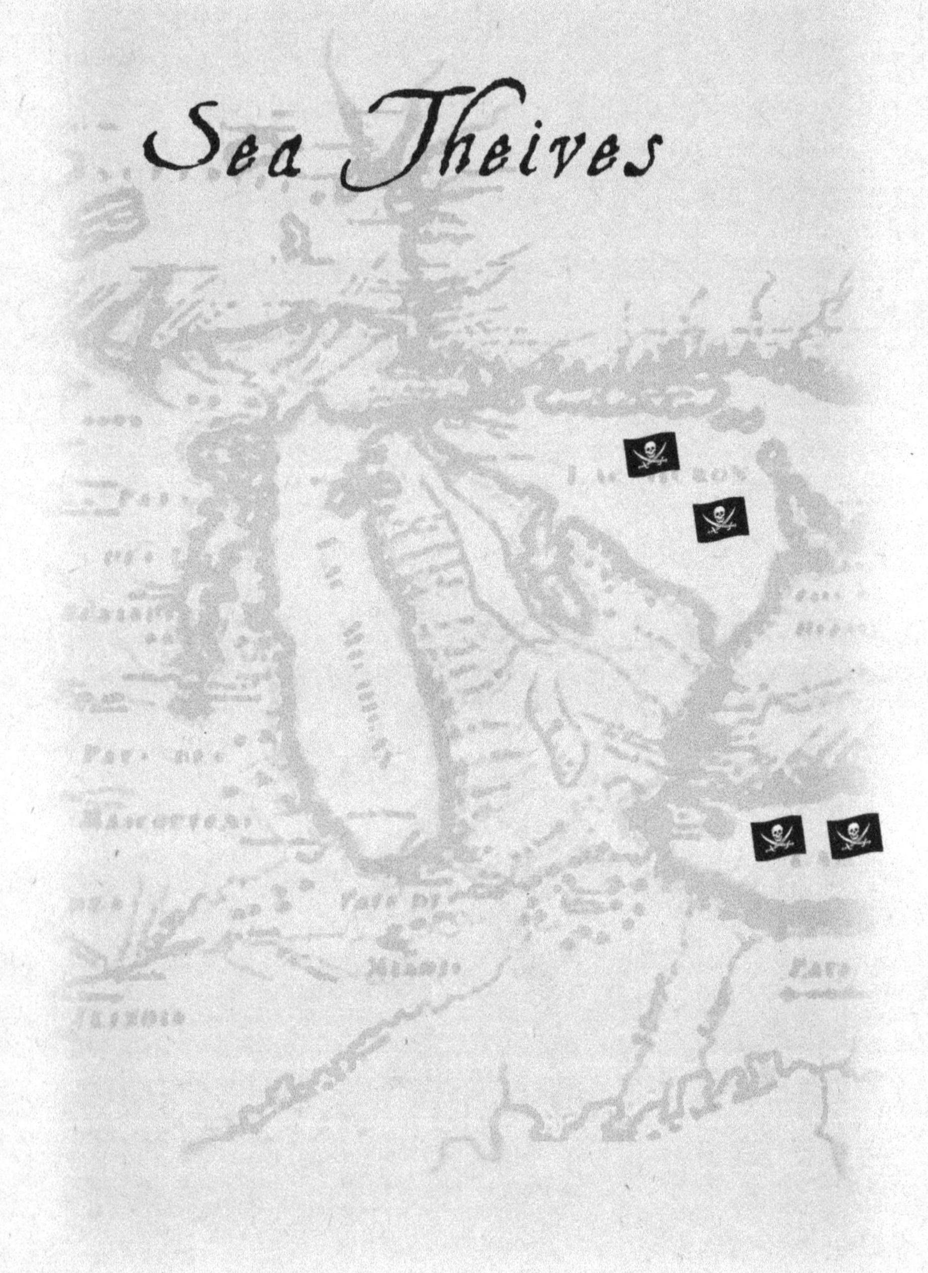

Fishing Pirates

After the American Revolution, Canadians in the north were wary about American aggression and a possible invasion from across the lakes. American and British tensions erupted in the form of the War of 1812. Originally Americans pressured the government to go to war, but neither side was ready financially. When war was declared, the first fort to fall was Fort Mackinac on Mackinac Island, Michigan. For the rest of the war much of the sea battles took place on Lake Erie and Lake Ontario. Years since the War of 1812, tensions between the United States and Canada were at a lakes length. Over time fishing businesses popped up on both sides of the lakes.

Fisherman would go where the largest population of fish was, even if that meant crossing the border into foreign waters. Many of the fishermen would obtain licenses in the state they resided in; however after crossing into Canadian waters their licenses were not legal. After discovering that Americans were crossing into their waters, Canadian officials began to chase down these fishing pirates. Arrests began to rise on the Canadian side with the Canadian officials seizing fish, boats and materials. On the American side officials would buy back the fishermen's boat and assist in the releasing of the fishing pirates. Needless to say, the Canadians were not without their fishing piracy. Canadians would also cross into American waters to fish. At first American officials did nothing about it until American fishermen began to complain.

As more American fisherman were arrested by Canadian authorities, these fisherman began to form a system to avoid capture. The Americans would cross into Canadian waters staying close to the border. When Canadian authorities were sighted the fisherman would signal the other fishing boats to head back across the border where it was safe. Once the Canadian authorities left the Americans would head back across the border.

As newly formed treaties were signed by both the American and Canadian governments to protect the Great Lakes, fish piracy began to die out as fewer fishermen crossed the border.

The Rumrunners

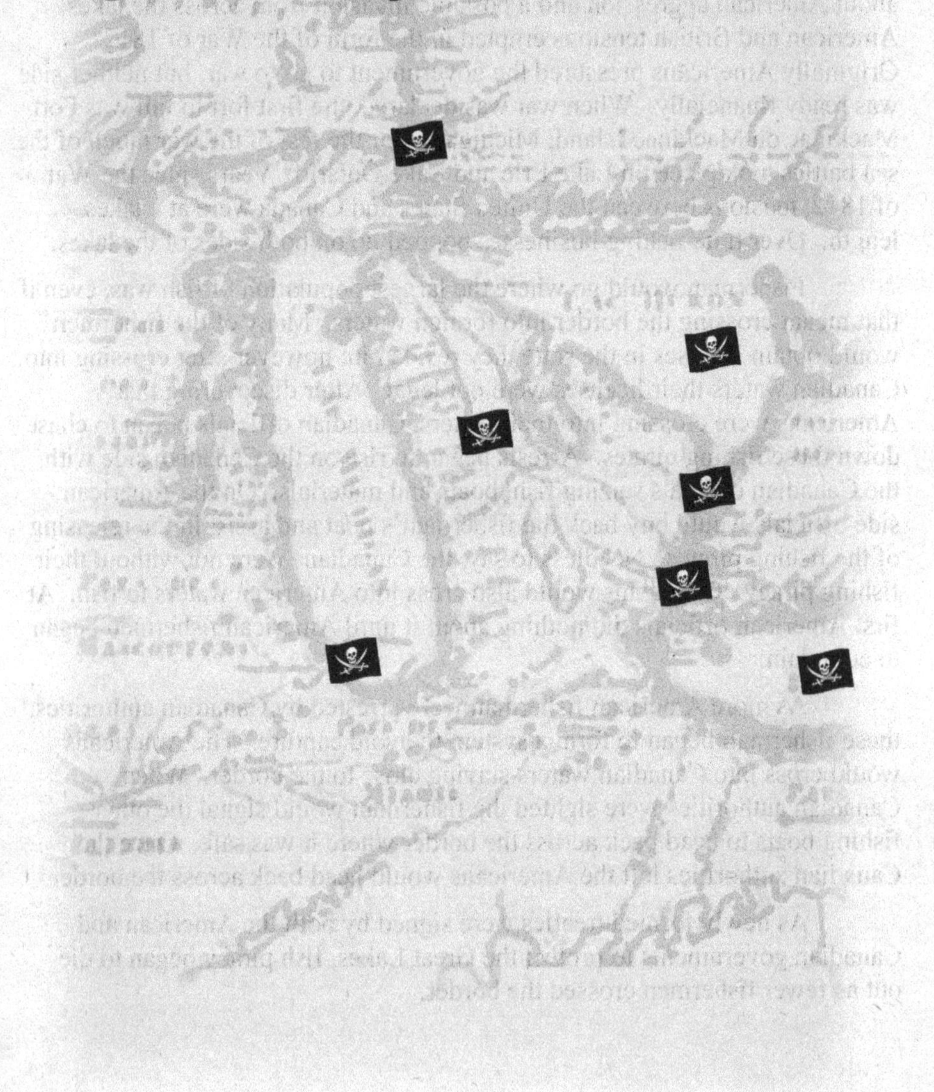

The Purple Gang

These Russian Jewish mobsters got their start in the Jewish section of the East Side of Detroit during the 1920's and the 1930's. Originally designed and founded by Sammie "Purple" Cohen, the leadership was passed onto the three Bernstein brothers who immigrated to Detroit from New York. The gang got its name The Purples for being a band of bad men like the purple on a bad steak. The gang began with petty robbery and extortion, but when Congress passed prohibition they quickly went into the distillery and brewing business. Over a short period of time the gang merged with another group known as the Oakland Sugar House Gang and both came under the authority of Abe Bernstein and were known as The Purple Gang. Upon the merger the Purple Gang began operations branching out into Canada and smuggling liquor across the Detroit River into Michigan. They referred to the Detroit River as "Our River" and reminded other Detroit gangs when they trespassed on it. No gang in their right mind would want to cross the Purples or else they would find themselves at the bottom of their river. Their number one buyer was none other than Al Capone of Chicago. The two operations drew so intense that a gang border was established near Grand Rapids. From the start "Big Al" entered Detroit looking to take control of what mobsters called The Funnel (referring to Detroit.) Capone was taken to a remote area by the Purples and was told to stay out of Detroit. Capone thought it wiser to do business with the Purples rather than make enemies out of them.

Over the years of prohibition, the Purples became known for their violent activities smuggling Canadian whiskey on Detroit's waterfront. Much of their operations took place on waterfronts throughout the Great Lakes smuggling whiskey as far north as Clare, Michigan and onto the waterfronts of Chicago. It was due to illegal activities on lakeshores and rivers that many claim were acts of piracy.

Gang members loading rum near the Detroit River.

On September 16, 1931 at 3:00 p.m. the Purples finally settled a grudge with three men that wouldn't listen to reason. The Purples had invited Hymie Paul, Joe "Nigger Joe" Lebowitz, both 31, and 28-year-old Joe "Izzy" Sutker to 1740 Collingwood, Apartment 211. The men arrived unarmed because they believed it to be a peace meeting, but the Purples had other plans. As a car horn outside gave the signal, the Purples opened fire on the three men killing them. Police reports suggested that the men were shot while attempting to run due to the many gun shots in their backs. Eye witnesses spotted men running out of the building into a 1930 Chrysler and driving off.

Wayne County Prosecutor Harry S. Toy ordered the round up of all the Purples; Detroit had had enough of the Purple Gang. Within 48 hours, working off of anonymous tips, the police dragnet arrested several top Purple Gang members. After an hour and a half of deliberations the jury had found three men guilty. Ray Bernstein, Irving Milberg and Harry Keywell were sent to a maximum security prison in Marquette, Michigan. The killings came to be known as the Collingwood Massacre, and as the gang's leaders went to prison many of the gang's members were dissolved into the underground national crime syndicate.

The Treasure of Poverty Island

X

The Lost Treasure of Poverty Island

There are several legends that surround Poverty Island but none have been confirmed. This isn't a pirate story nor is it truly known if pirates were involved but the lost treasure of Poverty Island is a story that many sailors and treasure hunters have been eager to find.

Poverty Island is a small island in Lake Michigan on the Michigan side of the inland sea. One legend holds that an American schooner with a crew of 60 men and 5 chests of gold aboard (during the time of American and English hostilities) was wrecked off the coast of the island. If the story is true it is estimated that the gold would be roughly worth 400 million dollars today.

Another legend tells that a crew of English was being chased by a French ship. Rather than lose their gold to the French when the ship would be overtaken, the English crew pushed 4 or 5 chests of gold overboard to the depths of Lake Michigan near the island.

Many have searched through records and legends to find the location of the gold near Poverty Island but with no avail. Others have attempted treasure hunting near the island with intent on finding the gold. Michigan is mostly famous for its copper and many think that gold doesn't exist in the state. However, Michigan has been known for hundreds of gold enriched sites. Gold has been discovered in thirty-three counties in the whole state of Michigan. In the late 1800's Michigan actually had a gold rush with as many as nine gold mines open with the first mine being opened in 1880 with the rush lasting until 1897. According to the United States Forest Service nearly every river in Michigan has shown signs of gold and nearly every gravel pit.

With the discovery of underground volcanic kimberlitic pipes under several areas of the state, it is believed that Michigan has the potential to hold the largest diamond mine in North America.

The Lost Treasure of Poverty Island

There are several legends that surround Poverty Island but none have been confirmed. This isn't a pirate story nor is it truly known if pirates were involved but the lost treasure of Poverty Island is a story that many sailors and treasure hunters have been eager to find.

Poverty Island is a small island in Lake Michigan on the Michigan side of the inland sea. One legend holds that an American schooner with a crew of 60 men and 5 chests of gold aboard (during the time of American and English hostilities) was wrecked off the coast of the island. If the story is true it is estimated that the gold would be roughly worth 400 million dollars today.

Another legend tells that a crew of English was being chased by a French ship. Rather than lose their gold to the French when the ship would be overtaken, the English crew pushed 4 or 5 chests of gold overboard to the depths of Lake Michigan near the island.

Many have searched through records and legends to find the location of the gold near Poverty Island but with no avail. Others have attempted treasure hunting near the island with intent on finding the gold. Michigan is mostly famous for its copper and many think that gold doesn't exist in the state. However, Michigan has been known for hundreds of gold enriched sites. Gold has been discovered in thirty-three counties in the whole state of Michigan. In the late 1800's Michigan actually had a gold rush with as many as nine gold mines open with the first mine being opened in 1889 with the rush lasting until 1897. According to the United States Forest Service nearly every river in Michigan has shown signs of gold and nearly every gravel pit.

With the discovery of underground volcanic kimberlite pipes under several areas of the state, it is believed that Michigan has the potential to hold the largest diamond mine in North America.

Pirates in the News

Historians are not the only people to keep records of pirates on the Great Lakes. Newspaper articles from Chicago to Buffalo record the robberies and pillages by pirates on the Great Lakes. There are many stories of lake and river pirates in the Great Lakes regions that newspapers recorded. Below are just a few of the stories.

The Buffalo Commercial Advertiser recorded the piracy of the PHILO PARSONS on March 20, 1865. The article describes the capture of the ship in September of 1864.

On March 10, 1838 the Kingston Chronicle & Gazette depicted an encounter with pirates on Point au Pelee Island on the Canadian side of the border. Two months later the Kinston Chronicle & Gazette placed another article on May 30, 1838 describing the SIR ROBERT PEEL Steamer, being destroyed during the morning by a band of pirates that called themselves Patriots at Well's Island within seven miles of French Creek.

On Tuesday, August 14, 1894 the Detroit Free Press reported six alleged pirates were arrested at Port Huron by Marshal Petit and arraigned before Commissioner Graves. William Johnson, William Murphy, William Cooper, Thomas Willis, Patrick McLaughlin and Grant Gray with their schooner the EMMA were considered to be river pirates and charged with attacking a vessel with intent to plunder. Prior on August 8th the Detroit Free Press informed the public that the crew of the EMMA would be charged with robbing a bumboatman on the high seas. The men were tried under the state law on the charge of robbery. Mr. Wilkins, who was the Assistant U. S. Attorney, interpreted the law provided by the Supreme Court on piracy in a famous Alaskan case. The law was in instituted in the case of the EMMA. Due to the Supreme Court ruling the Great Lakes were considered to be high seas justifying the ruling of piracy. The Free Press went on to state that the U.S. penalty for piracy was hanging. Canadian authorities had applied for extradition for the crew of the EMMA but U.S. authorities refused even though the crimes were committed on Canadian waters.

September 1, 1836, the Black Rock Advocate reported that they had run across some Detroit papers telling of a gang of gew-gawed gentry that were arrested by the Sheriff of St. Clair County and a crew of citizens on board the steamboat GEN. GRATIOT. The crew that was arrested claimed to be Mexican but wore uniforms of blue trimmed with red. They sailed an old black schooner without a name, which was towed into Black River where it was examined.

Tuesday September 15, 1885, the Detroit Post reported that river pirates had victimized the ship M.P. BARKALOW near Eighteenth Street on a Saturday night. The pirates had stolen a supply box that was worth $18.

November 15, 1877, the Detroit and Tribune ran a story about pirates on the Detroit River and St. Clair River that were captured. Their boat was captured with only one seaman aboard. The pirate's boat contained 150 bushels of barley that were stolen from a Henry Caswell, 60 bushels of oats that were stolen from Harsen's Island. The pirate boat was reported to have a supply of bags. Six bags were marked with an "R" in black paint, two were marked with a blue cross, and one was marked with the letters "W.I.L.".

The Authors

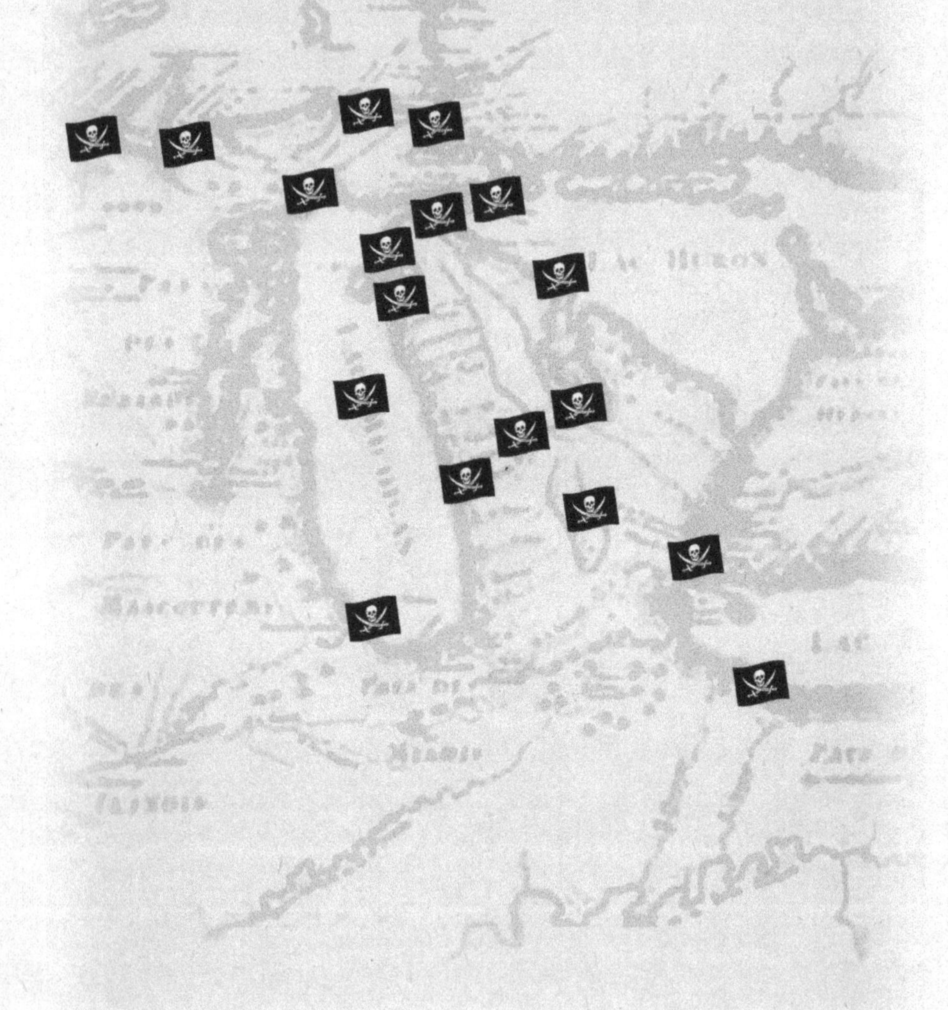

About the Authors

Greg and Nancy Haggart reside in Coleman, Michigan. They have been married since 2001 with their family of a yellow lab (Hunter) and kitty (Arwin).

Greg is a graduate of Mid Michigan Community College and currently attending TBI to receive a doctorate of theology. He also works for a major commercial printer and serves as the chairman of the board of the Well of Worship, Inc.

Nancy works for a Central Michigan newspaper company and serves as the Corporate Secretary of the Well of Worship, Inc.

Greg and Nancy are an adventurous couple with a true passion for God. They enjoy the great outdoors, ghost hunting, historical research, and spreading the gospel of Jesus Christ.

Bibliography

INTERNET

HYPERLINK http://www.apa.org/journals/webref.html

HYPERLINK http://en.wikipedia.org/wiki/Jos%C3%A9_Gaspar

HYPERLINK http://www.josegaspar.net/AboutJose.htm

HYPERLINK http://www.boatingfest.com/pirate.html

HYPERLINK http://en.wikipedia.org/wiki/USS_Michigan

HYPERLINK http://en.wikipedia.org/wiki/USS_Michigan_%281843%29

HYPERLINK http://en.wikipedia.org/wiki/Bully_Hayes

HYPERLINK http://www.janesoceania.com/restieaux_hayes/index.htm

HYPERLINK http://homepages.ihug.co.nz/~tonyf/hayes/index.html

HYPERLINK http://www.adb.online.anu.edu.au/biogs/A040413b.htm

HYPERLINK http://en.wikipedia.org/wiki/Jacob_Thompson

HYPERLINK http://www.suntimes.com/news/metro/422350,CST-NWS-pirate11.article

HYPERLINK
http://www.mied.uscourts.gov/_historical/newspdf/Court%20Legacy%2009-03.pdf

HYPERLINK http://usncsn.fateback.com/Indi_A_B/Individuals_A-B.html

HYPERLINK http://www.history.navy.mil/

HYPERLINK http://en.wikipedia.org/wiki/Colby_Pirates

HYPERLINK http://en.wikipedia.org/wiki/George_Colby

HYPERLINK http://www.answers.com/topic/colby-pirates

HYPERLINK http://www.bookrags.com/research/french-and-indian-war-legacy-of-aaw-01/

HYPERLINK http://music.musictnt.com/biography/sdmc_George_Colby

HYPERLINK http://road7.blogspot.com/2005/01/places-to-visit-or-why-i-love.html

HYPERLINK http://www.boatingfest.com/pirate.html

HYPERLINK http://www.janesoceania.com/restieaux_hayes/index.htm

HYPERLINK http://www.pohnpeiheaven.com/earlycontact18.htm

HYPERLINK http://www.piratesinfo.com/history/history.php

HYPERLINK http://en.wikipedia.org/wiki/Viking

HYPERLINK
http://www.michiganepic.org/lumbering/LumberingBriefHistory.html

HYPERLINK http://www.shgresources.com/mi/history/

HYPERLINK http://www.crimelibrary.com/gangsters_outlaws/gang/purple/1.html

HYPERLINK
http://info.detnews.com/history/story/index.cfm?id=183&category=life

HYPERLINK http://www.2manitowoc.com/biosF.html

BOOKS

Butts, Edward (2004). Outlaws of the Lakes: Bootlegging & Smuggling from the Colonial Times to Prohibition. Holt, Michigan: Thunder Bay Press

Stonehouse, Fredrick (2004). Great Lakes Crime: Murder, Mayhem, Booze & Broads.

Gwinn, Michigan: Avery Color Studios, Inc..

Powers, Tom (2002). Michigan Rogues, Desperados & Cut-Throats.

Davison, Michigan: Friede Publications

Konstam, Angus (1998). Pirates 1660-1730.

Osceola, WI: Osprey Publishing

Maynard, Christopher (1998). Pirates! Raiders of the High Seas.

New York, New York: DK Publishing, Inc.

Meek, Forrest B. (1976). Michigan's Timber Battleground: A History of Clare County: 1674-1900.

Clare, Michigan: Clare County Bicentennial Historical Committee

Clary, James (1981). Ladies of the Lakes.
Woolly Bear Productions, a unit of Michigan Natural Resources Magazine

Hivert-Carthew, Annick (1994). Cadillac and the Dawn of Detroit.
Davisburg, Michigan: Wilderness Adventure Books

MAGAZINES

Rosentreter, Roger L. (2003, November/December). The Island Kingdom of James Strang:
A history of Beaver Island under the rule of James Jesse Strang.
Michigan History Magazine, 80-82

CPSIA information can be obtained
at www.ICGtesting.com
Printed in the USA
LVHW091623030323
740510LV00036B/2055